I0835028

Copyright © 2021 by Matt Bodett

All rights reserved. This book or any portion thereof may not be reproduced or used in any manner whatsoever without the express written permission of the publisher except for the use of brief quotations in a book review and certain other noncommercial uses permitted by copyright law. For permission requests, write to the publisher at the address below.

Printed in the United States of America

First Printing, 2021

ISBN: 978-1-955498-99-9

Press Here
410 S Michigan Ave Suite 420
Chicago, IL 60605

www.mattbodett.com

rhetoric

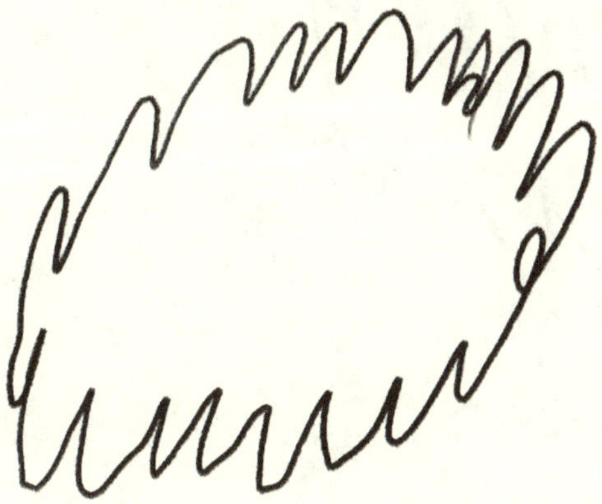

smoke

to open

top

plan

say

know

very

shared

alias

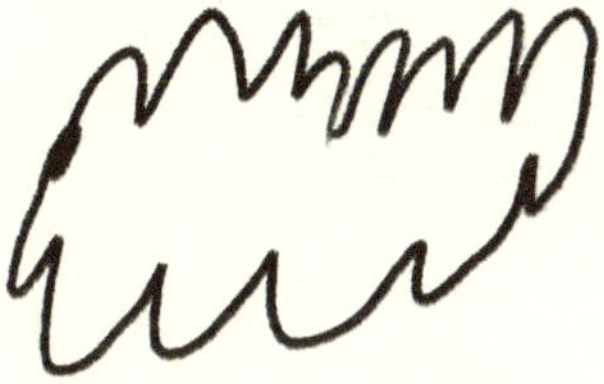

of

the

as

too

for

getting

tone as sky

cross

thres
hold

belong
ing

times
held

sample
names

Spent

911

911

em b r
ac e

folded
a w ay

back to

much

moment
s

catch waiting it

planned

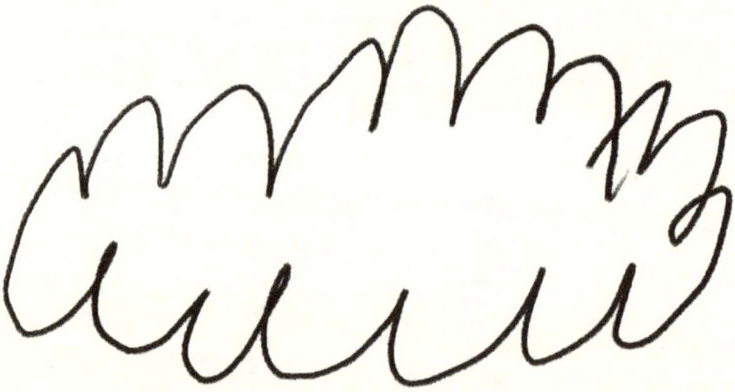

for it to
wait
me

too

much

all folt

years

promises

went

divine

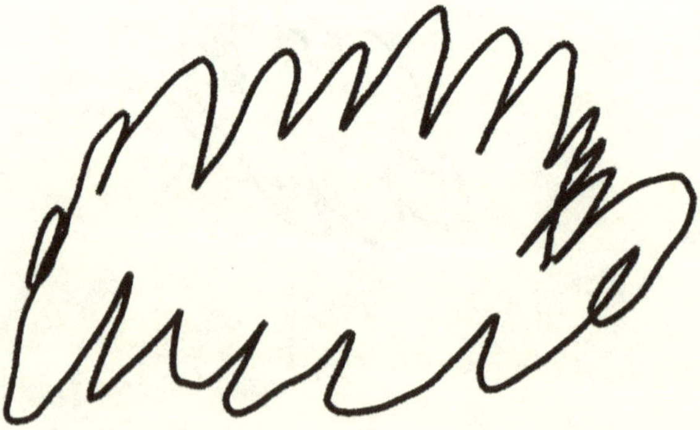

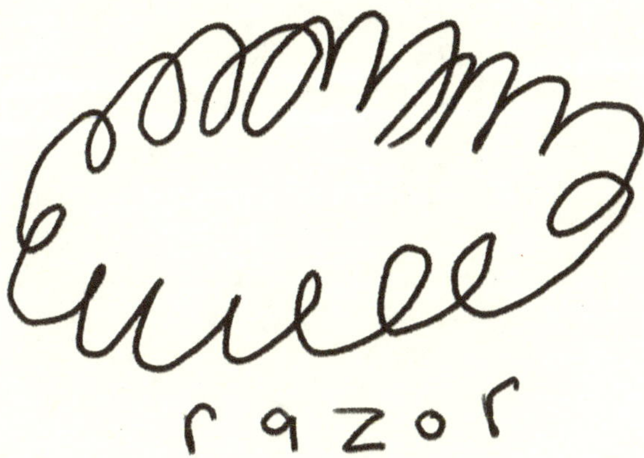

softet

crash and

relief

promise

too

good

about

enough

you knew

not told

flat care

hands
above

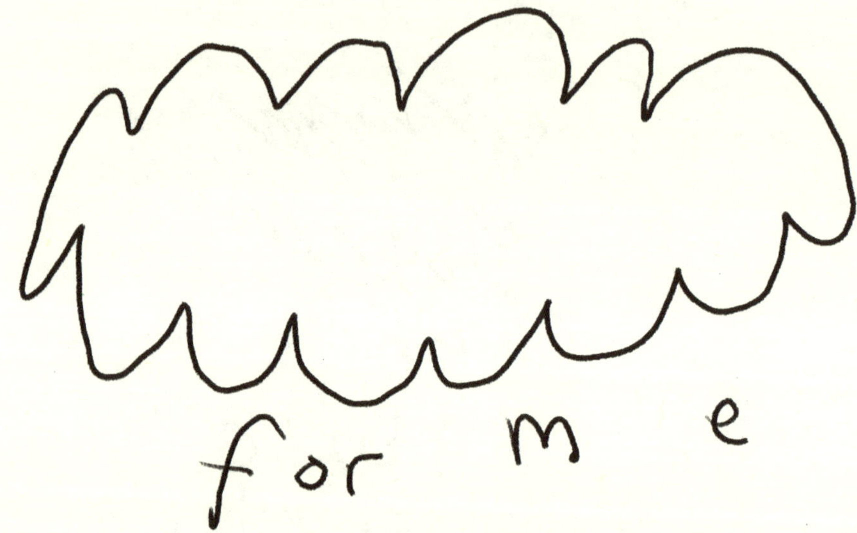
for me

catching
small
feed

pre
cise

moun

tain

shor es

with

take

pre

for

mis

ethical

know

hurry

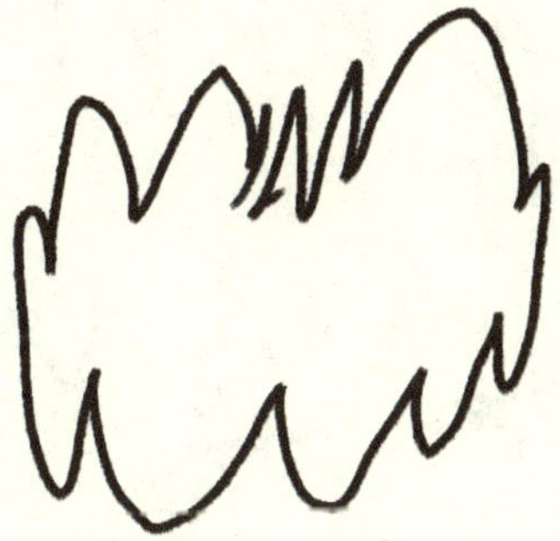

proven

~~proven~~

proven

911

sounds

we must

have

ways

voi ce

voic e
clear

voice

clears

voice

clearr

Limita

tions

---

sonic

very

end

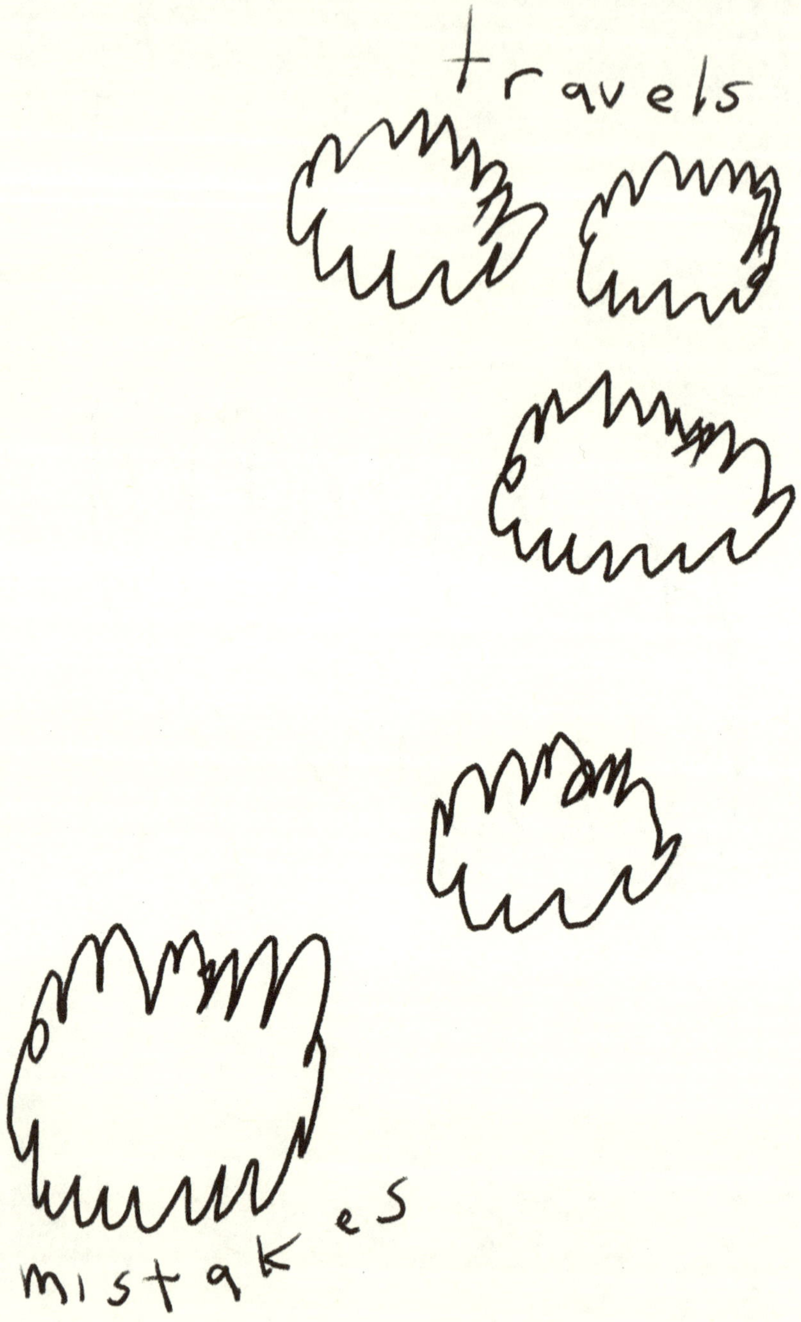

travels

mistakes

as water

spoiling

cost

lost

removed

la ck i ng

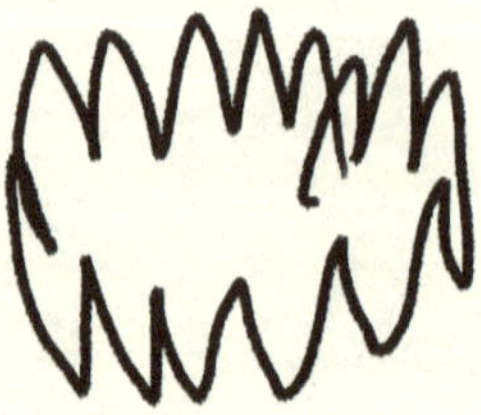

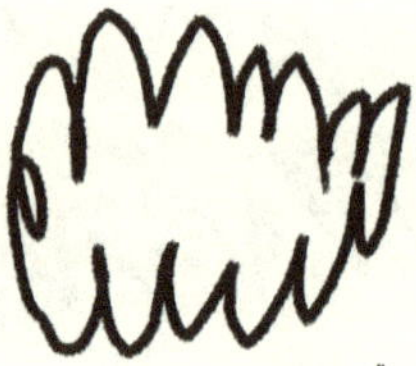

language

so little

left

now

points

to walk

skeptica

reproduced

reproduced

reproduced

object

you are

no longer

same

f o r m a l

realm

of

might be called

when

colded

pull or

using

extremely

disappeared

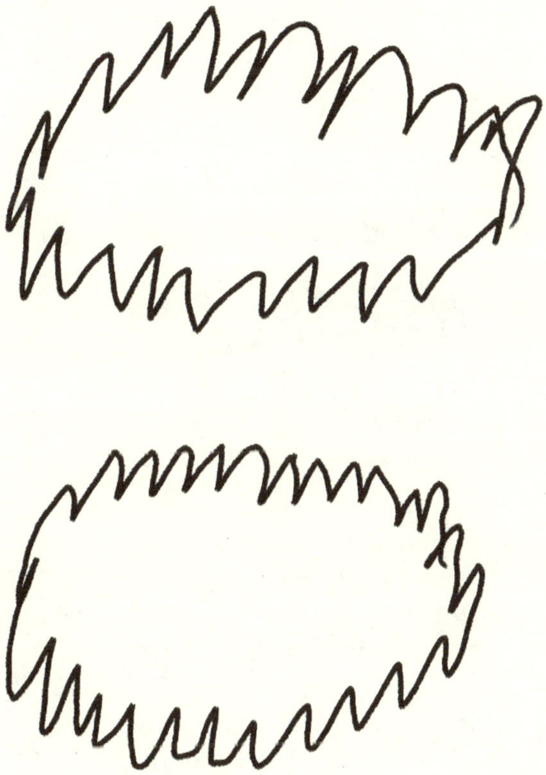

invest

ment

otherwise

diff

erence

re

present

ing

not

a story

through

un telling

void

power

be

not

19 WS

can

mediate

subjects

aff i rms

ful crum

even

ground

lost

ground

who is doing

haunted

knot

ed

a

way to

approach

weight

p a r t i c u l a r

emits

problems

a loss

language

to

to

that

which

wh

disrupts

an

other

not

based

on

rich

important

(rhythm)

variety
material

all

commun
icate

(all)

took

off

9.5

~~10+~~

performa nce

so

so

so

toolso

page

not

vaque

em bo d y

www.ingramcontent.com/pod-product-compliance
Lightning Source LLC
LaVergne TN
LVHW051018080826
845145LV00009B/2684

* 9 7 8 1 9 5 5 4 9 8 9 9 9 *